This book belongs to:

_____

Creatures
of the Deep

Sandy Creek

© 2010 Top That! Publishing plc
This 2011 edition published by Sandy Creek, by arrangement with Top That! Publishing plc

Sandy Creek
122 Fifth Avenue, New York, NY 10011
ISBN-13: 978-1-4351-3198-9
Printed and bound in Guangdong, China
Manufactured April 2011
Lot 1 3 5 7 9 10 8 6 4 2

CONTENTS

CONTENTS

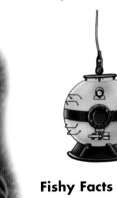

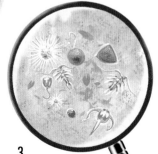

THE OCEAN AND THE WORLD

Earth was just another big rock flying through space 4.5 billion years ago. As the outer layer of our planet cooled to form a solid crust, water was released into the atmosphere. A giant ocean formed—and life began.

How did the first ocean create life

Life evolved in the ocean three billion years before it did on land. The first ocean was full of tiny chemical particles. Billions of years ago, these particles formed living cells. The first life forms were bacteria and algae that "ate" poisonous gases—like hydrogen sulphide and carbon dioxide—and "pooped" oxygen. These bacteria and algae made the world inhabitable for other creatures.

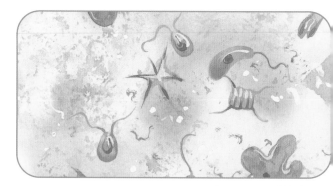

Earth's earliest life forms

What creatures lived in the primeval oceans

Had you been around 400 million years ago, you could have swam with armored fish and crab-like creatures called trilobites. When dinosaurs ruled Earth, 230 million years ago, marine reptiles called plesiosaurs swam in the oceans. The 65 ft (20 m) shark, called megalodon, ate whales for breakfast 20 million years ago!

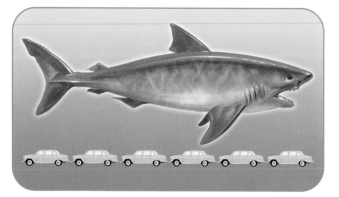

The megalodon shark grew up to 65 ft (20 m) long—that's as long as 6 cars!

A trilobite and an armored fish

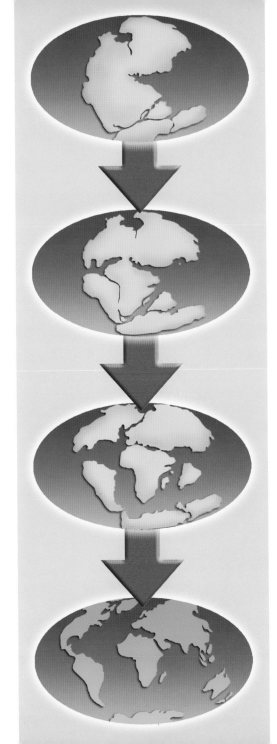

Until 250 million years ago, Earth's surface was a single landmass called Pangaea. Pangaea was surrounded on all sides by an enormous ocean called Panthalassa. Pangaea was torn apart by volcanic activity and eventually became today's continents. As this happened, Panthalassa also split into oceans.

Why are oceans important for life

Oceans are incredibly important for life on Earth because they provide most of the oxygen we breathe. Ocean currents keep the planet's temperature constant by absorbing the sun's warmth and moving it around the globe. Evaporation from the oceans helps to make rain—giving plants and animals water to drink. Scientists estimate that 230,000 forms of marine life are currently known, but there could be thousands more yet to be discovered.

What are today's oceans called

There are five oceans: the Pacific, the Atlantic, the Indian, the Arctic and the Southern. Together they cover just over 70% of Earth's surface in salt water. Sea water is salty because of minerals, like calcium carbonate, dissolved in it. Calcium carbonate is found in animals and in rocks and sand.

The single landmass, Pangaea, split into the continents we know today

LIVING IN THE OCEAN

The oceans are full of sea creatures of all different shapes and sizes. What's life like under water and how do living things survive down there?

What do sea creatures eat

Marine animals depend on each other for food. This can be demonstrated with a food chain. It works like this: predators eat other fish; these fish eat tiny creatures called plankton; and plankton eat bacteria. The smallest plankton feed on sunlight and produce the oxygen that keeps all other sea creatures alive.

How do sea creatures breathe

Sea creatures need oxygen, just like us. Luckily for them, water has oxygen dissolved in it. Most fish breathe through openings called "gills" on their heads. Sea water flows into the gills and over blood vessels. Oxygen "molecules" move from the water into the blood—and are carried around the fish's body.

Sea creatures need oxygen, just like us

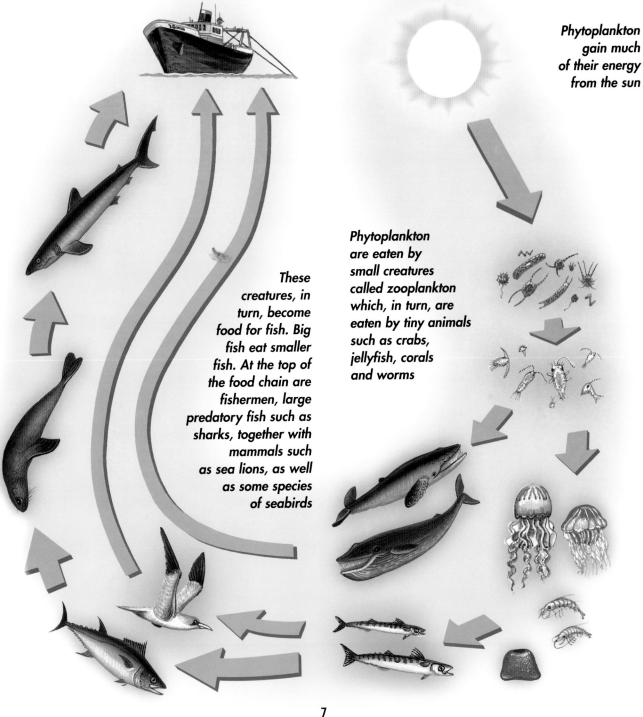

Phytoplankton gain much of their energy from the sun

Phytoplankton are eaten by small creatures called zooplankton which, in turn, are eaten by tiny animals such as crabs, jellyfish, corals and worms

These creatures, in turn, become food for fish. Big fish eat smaller fish. At the top of the food chain are fishermen, large predatory fish such as sharks, together with mammals such as sea lions, as well as some species of seabirds

How do marine animals protect themselves

Over thousands of generations, sea creatures have developed clever ways to protect themselves—and attack their "prey". Many animals use disguise or "camouflage" to hide from their potential predators, which enables them to blend into their surroundings. Others do the opposite: their bright colors are warnings to predators. Some use poison to attack prey or defend themselves.

Camouflaged sea creatures

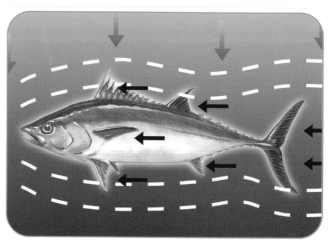

FACT FILE

The oceans provide 99% of the space available for life on Earth!

Why are fish that unusual shape

Fish have no legs or arms and have a curvy or "streamlined" shape. This makes it easier for them to move through water. As you may know from swimming, water is heavy—it weighs down or exerts "pressure" on you. Marine animals have a large body surface to withstand this pressure. Fish use their fins for swimming and, in some species, for gliding or crawling. They also help a fish move forward, turn and keep in an upright position.

A fish's streamlined body

THE SUNLIGHT ZONE

Dive into the sea and you are surrounded by soft, blue light. This water, near the surface, is full of life. This is the "epipelagic" or sunlight zone of the ocean.

Where is the sunlight zone

The sunlight zone stretches from the sea's surface to 656 ft (200 m) down—which is as far as sunlight can cut through water. Most sea creatures live here, including plankton. There is animal plankton and there is plant plankton. Plant plankton turns sunlight into oxygen by a process called "photosynthesis".

How do sea creatures stay afloat

If you live in sunny, warm waters, you certainly don't want to sink into the cold darkness below you. Sea creatures have large body surfaces that resist the water's natural tendency to push them downwards. Fish and whales also have oils or gases in their bodies to help with their buoyancy.

How far down can humans dive

Humans can't cope with sea water pressure. Our bodies collapse if we dive more than 229 ft (70 m) down—that's only a third of the way through the epipelagic zone! Humans can dive by holding their breath (free diving) or using apparatus (scuba diving) to help them breathe underwater. Scuba diving uses this apparatus in order to allow divers to stay under the water for longer. They have to go through many stages of training to ensure that they are safe. Many people dive for fun, but some dive professionally. For instance, scientific research, media coverage, and military and police work have all been carried out underwater.

Divers observe many beautiful sea animals

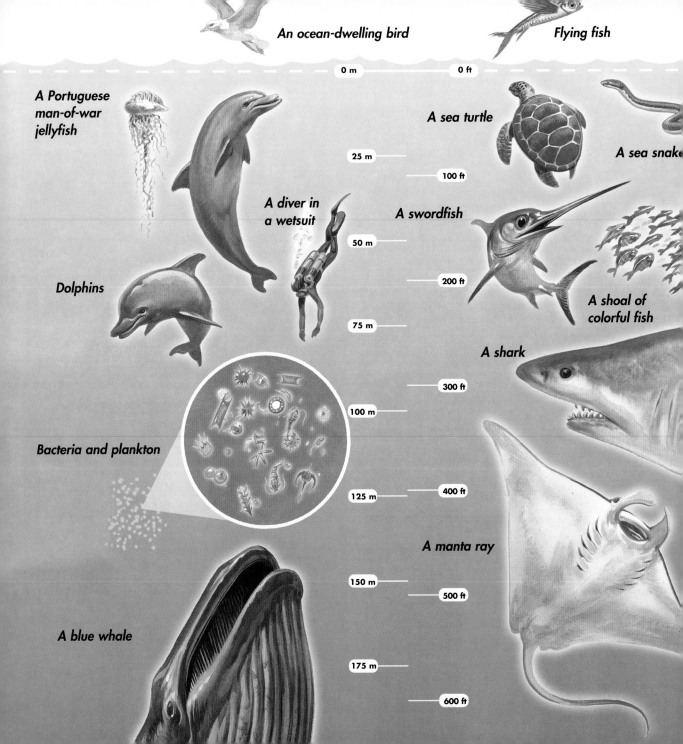

An ocean-dwelling bird

Flying fish

0 m   0 ft

A Portuguese
man-of-war
jellyfish

A sea turtle

A sea snake

25 m
100 ft

A diver in
a wetsuit

A swordfish

50 m
200 ft

Dolphins

75 m

A shoal of
colorful fish

A shark

300 ft

100 m

Bacteria and plankton

125 m   400 ft

A manta ray

150 m
500 ft

A blue whale

175 m

600 ft

Who lives here

Almost all the sea creatures you can think of live in the sunlight zone. There's fish, of course, like sharks, tuna and anchovies (one of the most common fish in the sea). There are also sea mammals like whales and sea lions, as well as squids, turtles and sea snakes.

Why does sunlight cause problems

The sunny sea is a great place to be—but there is one problem. Marine animals in sunlit waters can see what they want to eat, but this means that their predators can see them too! Sunlight zone dwellers are often a transparent bluish color, which helps them escape their enemies.

What do they eat

Plankton is the most popular food source in the entire ocean. Predatory marine animals like sharks, sperm whales and seals eat small fish. The sunlight zone is the perfect example of an "ecological system", in which different species live together and depend on each other for food, protection and survival.

How do fish hunt

All fish have a sense called the "lateral line" that runs down their backs and picks up vibrations in water. This line helps fish locate their prey and prevent collisions.

The lateral line runs down a fish's body

THE TWILIGHT ZONE

You'll need a special submarine to reach the "mesopelagic" or twilight zone. Light doesn't reach this far down very much—and the animals look really weird!

What's life like in the twilight zone

The twilight zone is cold and dark and there's little food because there are no plants to make oxygen. The twilight zone stretches from 656 to 3,300 ft (200 to 1,000 m)—at which point light is completely extinguished. There are fewer animals in this zone, due to the inhospitable environment.

How do they see in the dark

Some twilight zone dwellers have really large eyes that can see up to 3,281 ft (1,100 m) down in the gloom. Many have special chemicals in their bodies that make "bioluminescent" lights. These light the darkness, attract prey and provide camouflage from animals below them.

What do they eat

Most sea creatures here and below eat something called "marine snow". This is bits of decaying food and dead animal that drift down from the epipelagic zone above. Predators like pelican eels and viperfish have long, sharp teeth and expandable jaws so that they can eat animals much bigger than themselves!

Who lives in the twilight zone

Eels, octopuses, jellyfish and shrimp are common here. Other creatures like the lantern fish and the hatchet fish can be seen flashing on and off like traffic lights in the dark water. The firefly squid has three sets of lights on its almost "transparent" (meaning "see-through") body!

Why do fish go fishing

Here, food is so scarce that fish must conserve their energy. Predators don't waste energy chasing prey, they fish—hanging motionless in the water. Anglerfish use a glowing "fishing pole" stalk on their foreheads as a lure, while viperfish use lights in their mouths to guide prey into their stomachs.

Squid rising to the ocean's surface at night

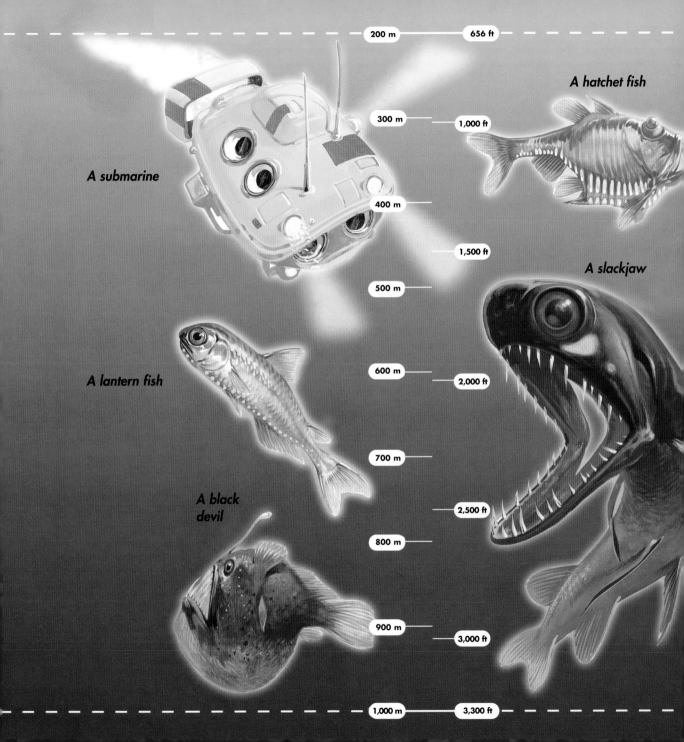

200 m   656 ft

A hatchet fish

300 m   1,000 ft

A submarine

400 m

1,500 ft

A slackjaw

500 m

A lantern fish

600 m   2,000 ft

700 m

2,500 ft

A black devil

800 m

900 m   3,000 ft

1,000 m   3,300 ft

THE MIDNIGHT ZONE

In the depths of the bathypelagic zone, night and day don't exist. The water is bone-chillingly cold and horrifying creatures haunt the blackness.

Where is the midnight zone

The midnight, or bathypelagic, zone is the biggest of the ocean zones. It stretches from 3,300 to 13,000 ft (1,000 to 4,000 m) below the ocean surface. The only food sources in the midnight zone are "marine snow" and predatory killing. The only light is bioluminescent.

Why do animals need camouflage in the dark

You might not think that animals need camouflage down here where it's pitch black—but they do! At these depths, many animals are red because, unlike black, it does not reflect in bioluminescent light. Therefore, red midnight zone dwellers become invisible to predators.

How do creatures cope with this harsh environment

Most midnight zone animals are extremely small. This reduces their need for food. They also have minimal skeletons, muscles and eyes—and don't swim very fast. They don't feel the water pressure because of gas or water in their bodies. They have thin skin, which absorbs oxygen easily.

Who lives in the midnight zone

It's a regular horror show here! There are big critters like the sperm whale—which chases giant squid—but it's the creepy creatures that run the place. They have names like vampire squid, dragonfish, ogrefish, pelican eels, football fish and ghost shark.

A viperfish

What are the creepiest creatures here

There are many bizarre-looking creatures in the midnight zone. Vampire squid drop down on their prey, lacerating them with sharp-spined tentacles. Anglerfish have teeth in their throats to stop prey escaping. Pelican eels, or umbrella mouth gulpers, have huge mouths, which they open to swallow fish much larger than themselves.

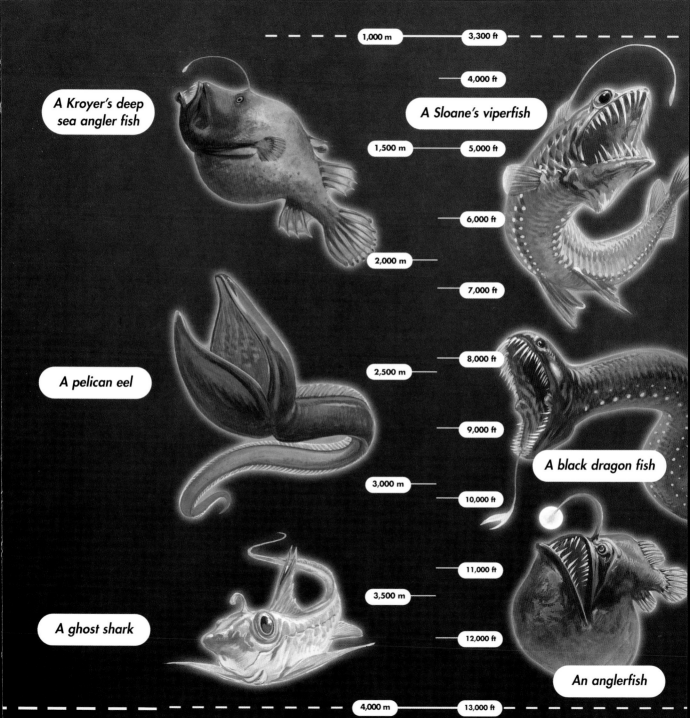

A Kroyer's deep sea angler fish

A Sloane's viperfish

A pelican eel

A black dragon fish

A ghost shark

An anglerfish

1,000 m — 3,300 ft

4,000 ft

1,500 m — 5,000 ft

6,000 ft

2,000 m

7,000 ft

2,500 m — 8,000 ft

9,000 ft

3,000 m

10,000 ft

11,000 ft

3,500 m

12,000 ft

4,000 m — 13,000 ft

THE SEA FLOOR

There's more life on the sea floor than in the two zones above it. If you want to live here, it helps if you like eating mud.

How deep down is the sea floor

The bottom of the sea is not a flat surface. The sea floor, which is also called the abyssalpelagic zone, can be anywhere from 13,000 to 19,680 ft (4,000 to 6,000 m) down. The abyssapelagic zone is muddier than a soccer field in November, but is also surprisingly full of life.

What is life on the sea floor like

The sea floor is made up of mud and ooze. Most of the creatures that live here are "invertebrates", which means that they lack backbones. The brittle starfish sinks into the mud but keep its tentacles out to catch food. Sea pigs get stuck in, searching the mud for earthworms.

Who swims over the sea floor

The transparent deep-water squid flounces through the water just above the muddy ooze, while the strange-looking flying sea cucumber uses its wings to zip about in all directions. The spindly tripod fish uses a set of extended fins as if they were legs—to avoid getting stuck in the mud.

Why is life cool down there

There is more food and oxygen available on the sea floor than in the two zones above. The ocean's leftovers can fall no further and collect here. This marine snow becomes a valuable food source. The near-freezing temperature has a strange effect: it actually extracts more oxygen from the water.

FACT FILE

Enormous sea spiders with 11 in. (30 cm) legs can be found scuttling along the sea floor.

Where can you warm up on the sea floor

This ocean environment isn't always near-freezing. A food chain has developed around the hot volcanic holes or "vents" that are scattered over the sea floor. Here, bacteria live off the poisonous volcanic gases. Small animals like snails and other "mollusks" eat the bacteria—and the snails are then eaten by crabs.

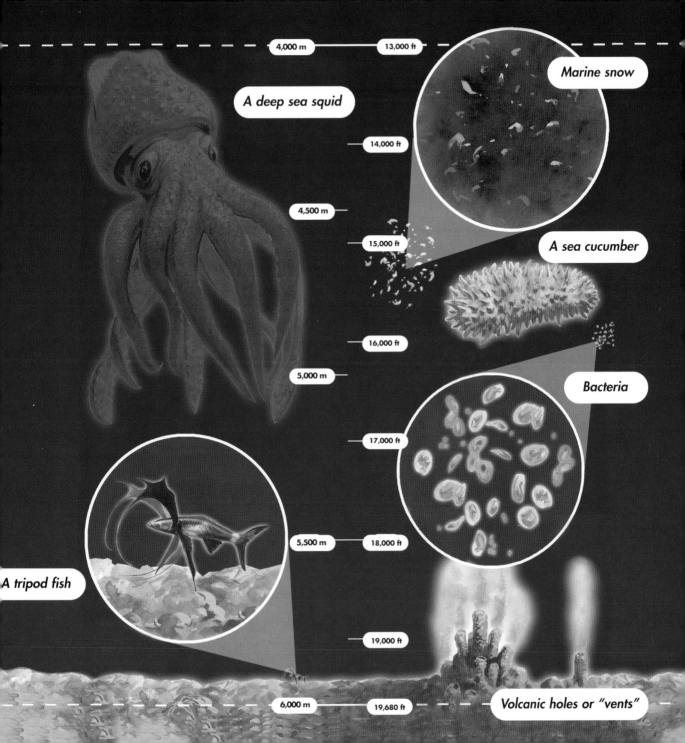

4,000 m   13,000 ft

Marine snow

A deep sea squid

14,000 ft

4,500 m

15,000 ft

A sea cucumber

16,000 ft

5,000 m

Bacteria

17,000 ft

A tripod fish

5,500 m   18,000 ft

19,000 ft

Volcanic holes or "vents"

6,000 m   19,680 ft

INTO THE ABYSS

There are immense rips in the ocean floor that lead even further down into darkness. Little is known about the creatures that live in this most extreme habitat on Earth.

What is the deepest point in the ocean

Trenches and canyons start to fall away from the ocean floor at 19,680 ft (6,000 m). The area between is the mysterious hadalpelagic zone—which is named after the ancient Greek word "hades"—meaning "hell". The Mariana Trench is the deepest point in the ocean. Located near Japan in the western Pacific Ocean, it forms a boundary between two tectonic plates (structure of Earth's crust). The trench is about 1,580 miles (2,550 km) long and reaches a depth of 36,198 ft (11,033 m) from the ocean's surface at Challenger Deep, a small slot at the southern end of the trench.

How high is the water pressure

Water is heavy—and the more there is on top of you, the heavier it gets. At the bottom of the hadalpelagic zone the water pressure is immense. If you went down there, it would feel like you had 48 jumbo jets pressing down on every part of your body!

Can we explore it further

Researchers and scientists are slowly learning more about deep-sea life. As modern technology allows us to explore further and deeper than ever before, new species of marine life are being discovered all the time. Who knows what other kinds of weird and wonderful sea creatures are lurking deep beneath the waves? Only three descents to the trench have ever been achieved. These were by special vessels, which could withstand enormous amounts of pressure. The first was a manned descent by a vessel called *Trieste* in 1960, the second was unmanned in 1995, and in 2009 *Nereus* reached the bottom of the trench. Scientists hope that *Nereus* will dive again and make new discoveries in the future.

FACT FILE

The Challenger Deep is named after the ship that made the first recordings of its depth, during its 1872–1876 expedition.

This really is the final frontier: scientists know much more about outer space than they do about deep-sea trenches.

The ocean floor
Height: 19,680 ft/6,000 m

Mont Blanc, France
Height: 15,771 ft/4,807 m

The Mariana Trench is deeper than the tallest buildings and mountains on Earth

Petronas Towers, Malaysia
Height: 1,483 ft /452 m

6,000 m   19,680 ft
20,000 ft
22,000 ft
7,000 m
24,000 ft
26,000 ft
8,000 m
28,000 ft
9,000 m
30,000 ft
32,000 ft
10,000 m
34,000 ft

Who lives here ?

Life gets its foot in the door everywhere—even in the most extreme and inhospitable places. The vessels that descended to the trench collected data and information on the life forms that they found. In spite of the pressure and temperature, starfish and tube worms have been found at these depths. On the sea floor, tube worms live near the volcanic vents, along with gigantic clams and mussels.

Starfish, tube worms, clams and mussels can live at these great depths

What's a tube worm ?

Tube worms are very basic "organisms"—but can be bigger than a human. They are up to 8 ft (3 m) long and live in tubes attached to rocks. They have very simple bodies, without eyes, mouths, intestines or stomachs. They are "hosts" to the bacteria that turn volcanic gases into sea food. Scientists believe that tube worms can live for up to hundreds of years.

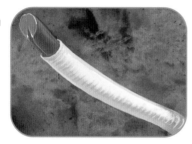

A tube worm

What are ROVs ?

Sea trenches can be as big as canyons and are always incredibly deep. No human has ever seen the bottom of a trench. It is hard to get information about trenches because even the most modern unmanned submarines— called ROVs or "remotely operated vehicles"— are difficult to maneuvre in tight spaces.

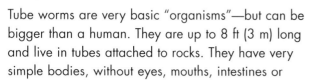

An unmanned submarine

LIVING IN PARADISE

In the warm, tropical waters off the coasts of Africa, India and Australia are some of the richest habitats in the seas: coral reefs that pulse and teem with colorful life.

Who lives in coral reefs

The coral reef is the greatest habitat—which means "living space"—in the whole ocean. The reef is usually a small area, but hundreds of species live there. You will find angelfish nibbling on sponges, pufferfish bloating themselves with water, sharks, parrotfish, crabs, turtles and sea snakes.

Where can you live on a reef

Some Caribbean islands are coral reefs that have been pushed out of the sea by volcanic activity. Coral reefs also grow around extinct ocean volcanoes. The reef rises up as the volcano slowly sinks into the sea. The circular island or "atoll" formed has a big hole in the middle.

A volcanic island

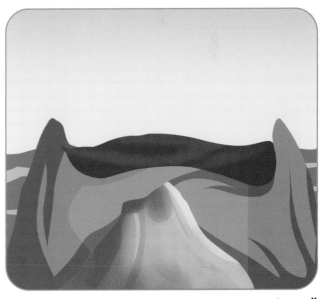

An atoll

What are clownfish ?

Colorful clownfish live amongst anemones, fish-eating animals that look like plants and have hundreds of poisonous tentacles. The anemone protects the clownfish from predators, while the clownfish cleans the anemone. This "helping-each-other-out" is called "symbiosis"—it's what coral reefs are all about.

A white-tipped reef shark

What are coral reefs ?

Coral reefs are huge masses of tiny tentacled animals called coral polyps. Young coral polyps settle on rocks and stay there for the rest of their lives. When a polyp dies, another grows on its chalky skeleton. Over thousands of years, the mass of skeletons turns into a reef.

A puffer fish

Parrotfish

Why are reefs dying ?

Coral reefs are dying because of industrial water pollution, reef tourism and "sedimentation". This is when sand covers the reef and kills coral by depriving it of sunlight. Reefs are also losing their beautiful colors. This is because a disease is killing the bacteria that give coral polyps bright colors.

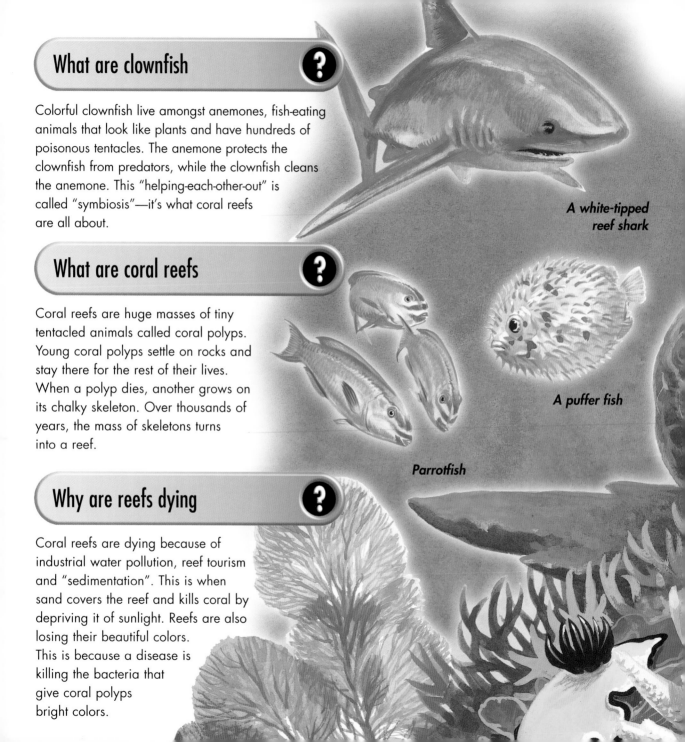

FACT FILE

Conchs are a group of mollusks with shells. The queen conch has a beautiful spiral shell that's lined in pink and up to 1 ft (30 cm) long. It is made from sea water minerals.

A sea snake

Clownfish

OCEAN OF ICE

The Arctic may look like a cold, white desert, but under—and on top of—the ice there's a huge amount of sea life, from orcas to furry seals.

Where can animals walk on the ocean

Usually an ocean surrounds a landmass, but in the case of the Arctic Ocean the ocean itself is actually the Arctic! The Arctic is a frozen ocean, which is totally covered with ice for most of the year. Mammals like seals, walruses and polar bears enter the sea to feed, but live and give birth on the ice itself.

Why is there so much food here

During the summer months, some of the Arctic ice melts and there is constant daylight. This allows plankton to "photosynthesize" all the time. This plankton explosion attracts billions of fish looking for food. The fish then attract seals and whales from thousands of miles away.

Seals

A walrus

Orcas

What creatures inhabit this ocean of ice

Harp and northern fur seals are some of the cutest inhabitants. Walruses with 3-ft (1-m) tusks sunbathe on the ice. The largest fish is the Greenland shark—it can grow up to 21 ft (6.5 m) long and has bioluminescent eyes. The Greenland shark can bust a hole through ice with its nose.

What famous whales live in the Arctic

The narwhal looks like a mix between a small submarine and a unicorn! Its tusk is 10 ft (3 m) long and is used for communicating with and fighting other narwhals. The smiling beluga whale makes so many funny chatters and clicks—even above the water—that it is often called the "sea canary".

A walrus on the ice

Polar bears

A Greenland shark

Narwhal whales

THE BIG BITE

Sharks have been around since long before the dinosaurs. There are 368 species and they live in every ocean at almost every depth.

Why do sharks attack humans

Few species of sharks attack humans—only the great white, tiger, bull and oceanic whitetip sharks do. They may mistake people for their favorite supper, seals. Sharks attack about 100 people each year.

What do sharks eat

Many sharks are carnivores that eat fish, squid, seals and sea lions. Flat sharks hide in the sand on the sea floor and pounce on crabs and clams. Larger sharks swim with their huge mouths open to collect plankton.

An Atlantic angel shark

4 ft/1.2 m

A blue shark

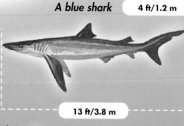

13 ft/3.8 m

A great white shark

20 ft/6 m

A basking shark

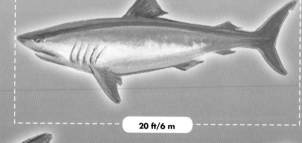

40 ft/12.2 m

Sharks are perfect predators. They are built to hunt and kill. Sharks have up to 3,000 teeth set in five rows. These teeth are triangular and sharp, with serrated edges —just right for taking big bites. When one tooth falls out, another takes its place.

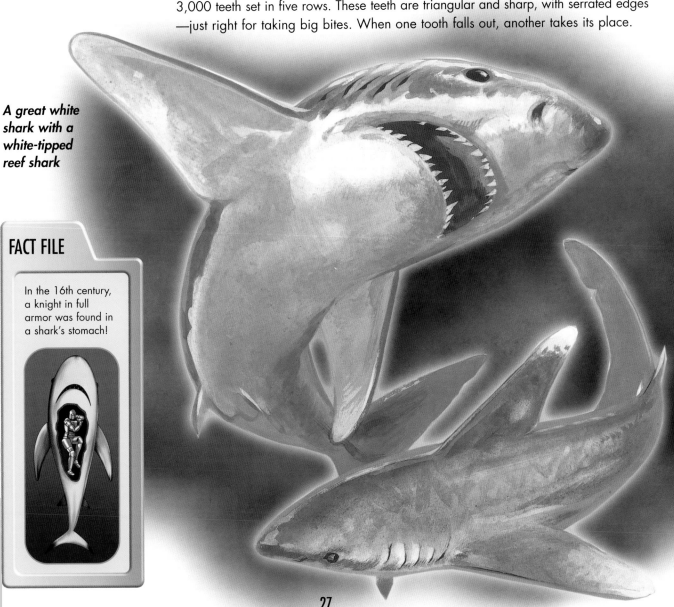

A great white shark with a white-tipped reef shark

FACT FILE

In the 16th century, a knight in full armor was found in a shark's stomach!

How do sharks hunt ?

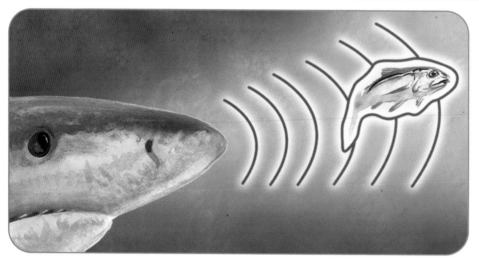

Sharks can sense lunch from more than a kilometer away. Unlike us, they can hear and smell really well underwater. They are also able to see pretty well—and use their special fish sense, the lateral line system (and extra electrical sense organs called an ampullae) to home in on their unlucky victims.

A shark stalks its victim

Why are many sharks blue ?

Shark camouflage is called countershading and makes sneaking up on prey easy. The top of the shark is blue, making it difficult to see from above, because it blends into the water below it. The shark's white belly makes it difficult to see from below, against the lighter water above it.

A shark's underside coloring (top) and upperside (bottom)

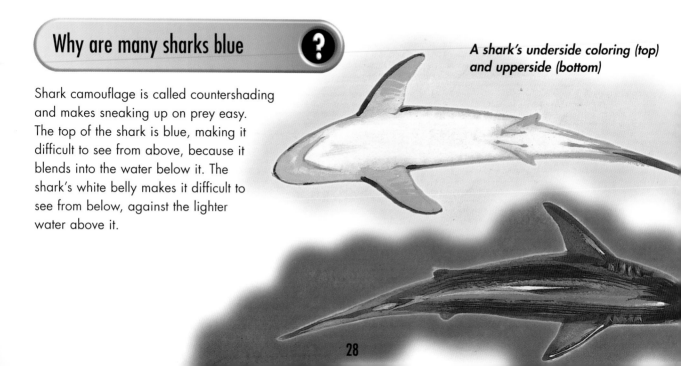

ROYALTY OF THE DEEP

Whales are one of the most intelligent and majestic creatures ever to live on Earth. They are also the only mammals that spend their whole lives in the open oceans.

What do whales eat

There are two types of whale. Whales with teeth, such as sperm whales and killer whales (or orcas), eat fish and squid. Other species, like blue whales, gray whales and humpback whales have filters in their mouths called baleen. With these filters, baleen whales sieve the water for tiny shrimp called krill.

Where do whales live

Whales live in all the oceans, near the surface. They dive for food. Sperm whales can dive for an hour, all the way down to 10,000 ft (3,048 m). Whales often live in large groups called "pods". They make long migrations in search of food: gray whales travel 12,500 miles (20,000 km) every year.

Why are many species endangered

For many centuries, humans have hunted whales for food and for the rich oil found in their bodies. This oil was used for burning in lamps. Other substances found inside some whales—like ambergris (a waxy substance)—were used to make perfume. Now many species are in danger of dying out and are protected by international law.

What is the biggest whale

The blue whale is the largest mammal in the world, weighing a huge 165 tons and measuring up to 105 ft (35 m) long. During the first seven months of its life, a calf will drink approx 88 gallons (400 liters) of milk every day, meaning it grows very quickly!

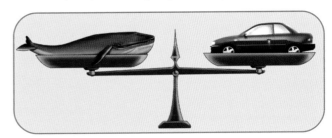

Newborn blue whales weigh 2.75 tons!

FACT FILE

Whales sing to each other underwater. These songs can travel for miles. Different whale pods sing very different songs. Whales with teeth also emit clicking sounds to detect prey. The sound waves bounce off the prey and return to the whale, who then knows exactly where the next meal is.

What is a whale song

Some species of whale, for example the humpback whale, make a pattern of regular sounds. It is not known for certain as to why the whales make these sounds, although it is thought that it could be to attract a mate and also to communicate with other whales, due to lack of sight and smell underwater.

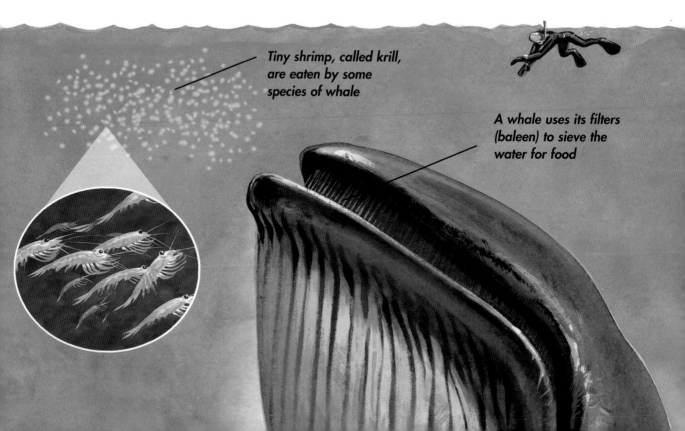

Tiny shrimp, called krill, are eaten by some species of whale

A whale uses its filters (baleen) to sieve the water for food

FACT FILE

After diving, whales clear the blowholes which take air to their lungs—shooting a water spout 50 ft (15 m) into the air—the same as the height of 8 people end to end.

What is breaching ?

Whales like to jump out of the water and bellyflop back down, known as breaching. They also like to stick their tails out of the sea and slap the water very hard. Many reasons have been suggested by scientists for this behavior, from making noise to scare prey to dominance, courting and warning in a group.

A whale shoots water out of its lungs through its blowhole

OUR BEST FRIENDS?

Dolphins are famous for being intelligent and friendly. You can swim with a 1,000 dolphins and they'll be as interested in you as you are in them!

How do dolphins talk

Dolphins like to whistle lots and stroke each other with their flippers. Dolphin moms teach each of their young a unique whistle. So when two dolphins meet, they are saying "hi" and telling the other dolphin their name. Scientists think humans can talk to dolphins—by turning words into whistles.

What is the major cause of dolphin deaths

In recent years, almost five million dolphins have been trapped and drowned in the enormous "drift nets" that are set to catch tuna. Many cans of tuna have "dolphin friendly" labels. This means that the tuna was caught in nets that allow dolphins to escape.

Dolphins are able to communicate with each other by whistling

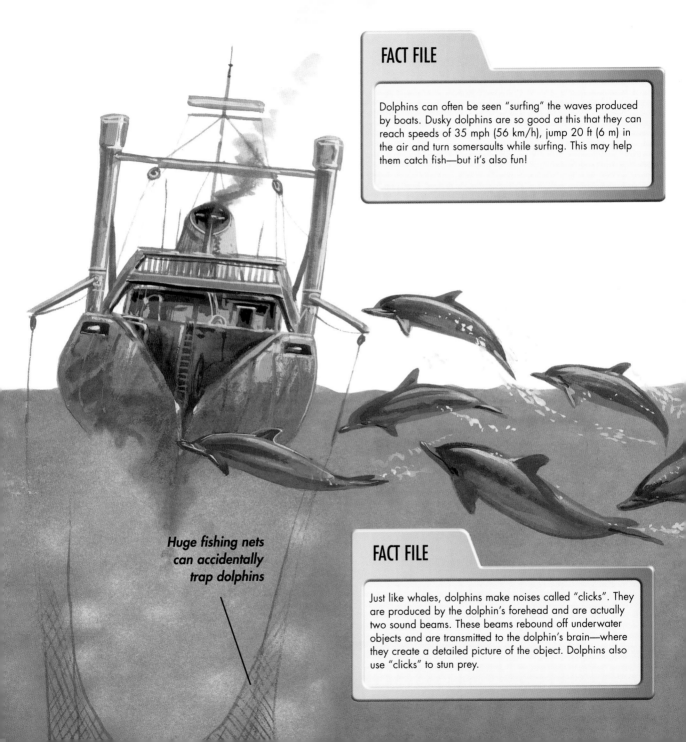

FACT FILE

Dolphins can often be seen "surfing" the waves produced by boats. Dusky dolphins are so good at this that they can reach speeds of 35 mph (56 km/h), jump 20 ft (6 m) in the air and turn somersaults while surfing. This may help them catch fish—but it's also fun!

Huge fishing nets can accidentally trap dolphins

FACT FILE

Just like whales, dolphins make noises called "clicks". They are produced by the dolphin's forehead and are actually two sound beams. These beams rebound off underwater objects and are transmitted to the dolphin's brain—where they create a detailed picture of the object. Dolphins also use "clicks" to stun prey.

OCEAN GLIDERS

Rays are amazingly graceful flat fish that glide over reefs and the sea floor. They are related to sharks and are found in all oceans, often in very large groups.

Why do rays look so strange

Rays look as though they've been squashed! They have fins that have melted into their flat bodies to form disks. Rays also have long tails. The ray's skeleton is made from cartilage. The skeleton and the disk are great for gliding through water—and for hiding on the sea bed waiting for prey.

Rays have flat bodies

How do rays swim

Rays swim very differently from other fish. The tips of their powerful, wing-like fins ripple and flap, allowing them to glide gracefully through water. Some rays, like the mangrove whipray and the manta, can even jump out of the water.

FACT FILE

Manta rays are curious and like to swim with humans —they especially like the bubbles from scuba-diving equipment and will also pop up near boats.

Rays can even jump out of the water

Why do stingrays attack humans

Because stingrays are flat and often hidden on the sea floor, people sometimes step on them. The stingray then lashes its whip-like tail, which has serrated, venomous spines. Humans can have heart attacks after being stung. Always "shuffle" through shallow, tropical waters to avoid being stung by a buried stingray.

Stingrays can hide on the sea floor

How big do rays get

The manta ray is the largest ray. It looks like a space-ship and can be 29.5 ft (9 m) wide and weigh many tons. Mantas eat plankton, funneling food into their mouth while they swim. They use the two flaps near their eyes like bendy chopsticks, to push food towards their mouths.

How do electric rays hunt

It's not the tail of the electric ray that you have to watch out for. It is the muscles in its head that produce a large electric current—of up to 220 volts! The ray drifts over fish and then zaps them. The ray wraps itself around the fish to concentrate the electric field.

An electric ray

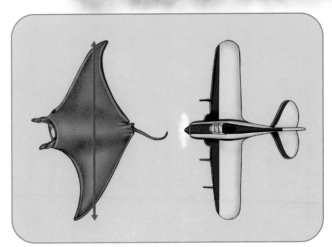

A manta ray can be as large as a plane

SPINELESS GENIUS

They writhe and wriggle through the ocean, but squid and octopuses are really clever when it comes to staying out of trouble.

What are squid and octopuses

Squid and octopuses are sometimes described as "humans without bones". They seem to be all tentacles and a big head. They don't have skeletons, which is why they move through the water in such a funny way. They do have highly advanced nervous systems. Squid have ten tentacles, octopuses have eight.

How do octopuses swim

Octopuses and squid are pretty unusual because they both use jet propulsion to swim. They suck in water through an opening in the back of their heads, then force it out through siphons on the sides of their heads. They can speed along at up to 23 mph (37 km/h).

FACT FILE

Some squid can jump 40 ft (12 m) out of the water to escape predators.

Each octopus tentacle has 240 suction cups on it for grip.

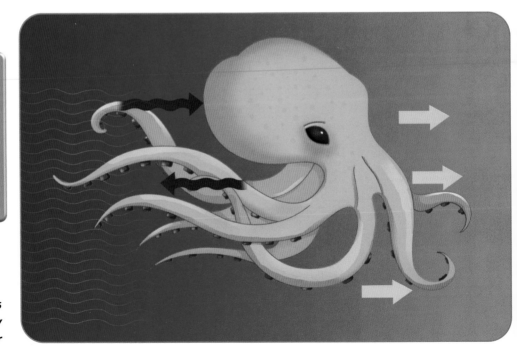

An octopus propels its body through the water

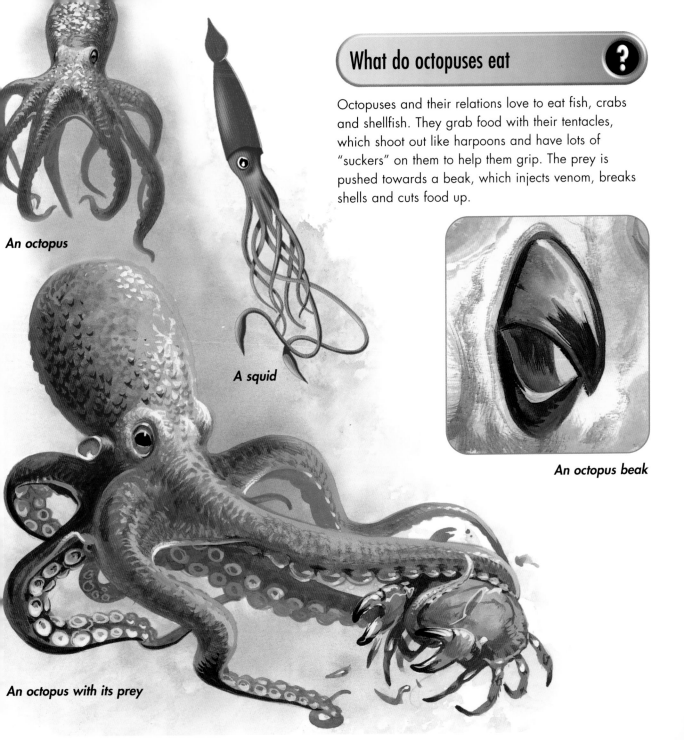

An octopus

A squid

What do octopuses eat ?

Octopuses and their relations love to eat fish, crabs and shellfish. They grab food with their tentacles, which shoot out like harpoons and have lots of "suckers" on them to help them grip. The prey is pushed towards a beak, which injects venom, breaks shells and cuts food up.

An octopus beak

An octopus with its prey

How do they avoid predators

So many animals eat squid and their cousins that they need to have very good defences. Many octopuses can change color to camouflage themselves or to frighten predators. Squid and octopuses are also famous for being able to squirt black ink at enemies. Some deep-sea species are transparent, which makes them almost invisible.

A squid squirts black ink from its body

Where do giant squid live

Giant squid live between 700 ft (200 m) and 13,300 ft (4,000 m) down. They are not as monstrous as they look in films—but they can be 60 ft (18 m) long. Giant squid have been known to fight with sperm whales nearer the surface; many sperm whales have sucker scars on their skin.

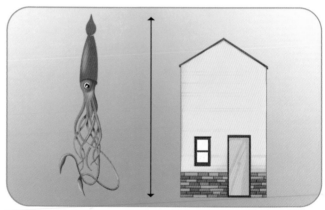

A giant squid can be as long as a house is high

A giant squid uses its suction cups to fight with a whale

FACT FILE

Octopuses live in caves and are very proud of their habitats: they use their siphons to squirt debris out of their homes after they have eaten.

COLD-BLOODED KILLERS

Speed, power, adaptability, sharp senses and sharper teeth—these are what make a perfect predator. In the sea, where most creatures are cold-blooded, size really doesn't count.

Who is the best-adapted predator

The most successful animals have adapted really well to their environments. The nudibranch takes this a step further—it actually adapts what it eats. This small, slow-moving sea snail eats jellyfish and sea anemones. The nudibranch incorporates their venoms and stings into its own body defenses to use against predators!

FACT FILE

The viperfish (below) impales prey on its oversized fangs after slamming into it at high speeds.

A nudibranch

A jellyfish

A sea anemone

Why do sharp senses help

The more precisely a predator tracks prey, the quicker it can kill and eat. Using its spade-shaped head, the hammerhead shark can detect a drop of blood in 22 gallons (100 liters) of water. The hammerhead swims towards dinner shaking its head. This tells it exactly where the target is.

How does the fiercest predator attack

The great barracuda lives on coral reefs. It is stealthy and lightning quick, with dagger-like fangs that tear, slash and slice. The barracuda's long body is flexible, allowing it to charge fast at its prey through twisting reefs. The barracuda has attacked swimmers—it is attracted to shiny bathing suits—mistaking them for prey.

A mantis shrimp

Which shark is the most dangerous

Great white sharks have a bad reputation, but they hardly ever attack people because they live in the deep ocean. The bull shark, however, swims near beaches. It is very bad-tempered and will attack anything. The bull shark can even swim up rivers and jump over rapids into lakes.

A bull shark

Who is the fastest predator

The 8 in. (20 cm) mantis shrimp is the fastest predator on Earth. It spears or smashes prey with a concealed, reinforced forearm. The strike is as fast (8 milliseconds!) and as powerful as a bullet. The mantis shrimp is a real pest in aquariums—it is always breaking the toughened glass.

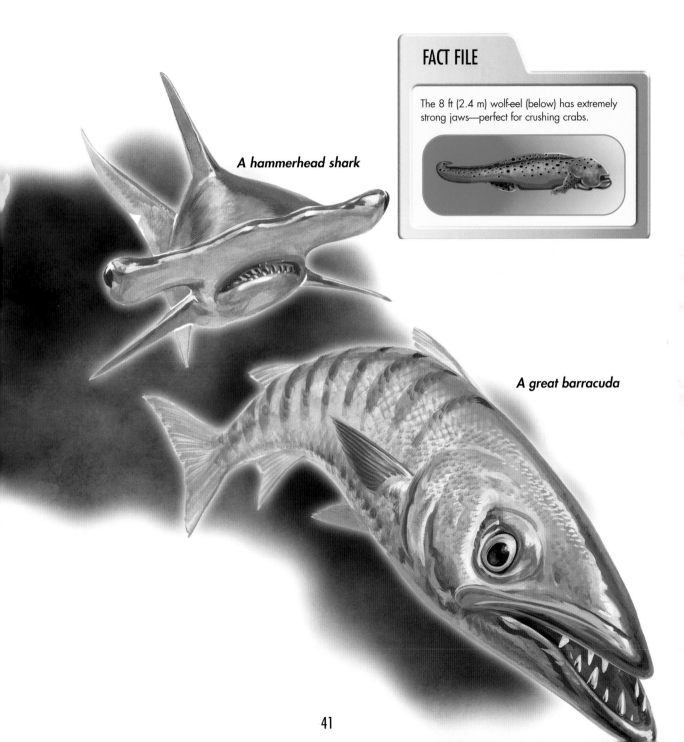

A hammerhead shark

A great barracuda

THE BIG ONES

Being one of the biggest creatures in the sea isn't easy. You may not have many predators, but feeding yourself becomes a full-time job.

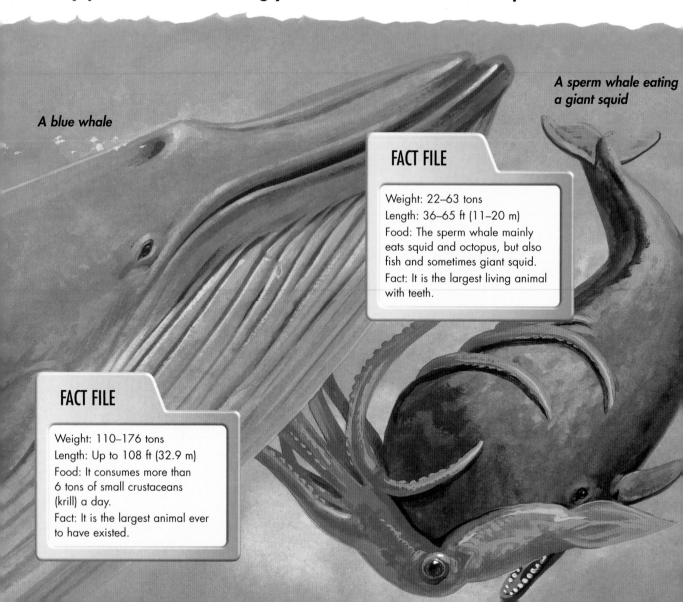

A blue whale

A sperm whale eating a giant squid

FACT FILE

Weight: 22–63 tons
Length: 36–65 ft (11–20 m)
Food: The sperm whale mainly eats squid and octopus, but also fish and sometimes giant squid.
Fact: It is the largest living animal with teeth.

FACT FILE

Weight: 110–176 tons
Length: Up to 108 ft (32.9 m)
Food: It consumes more than 6 tons of small crustaceans (krill) a day.
Fact: It is the largest animal ever to have existed.

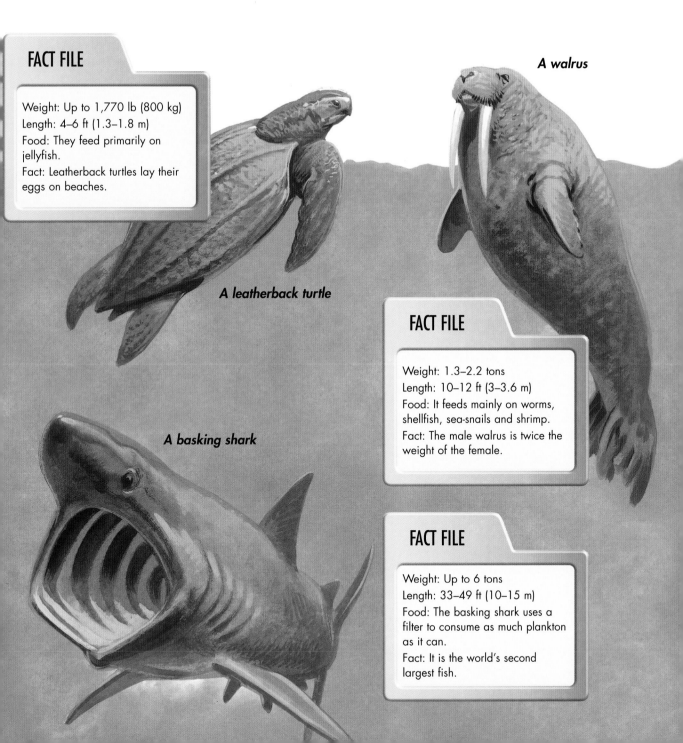

FACT FILE

Weight: Up to 1,770 lb (800 kg)
Length: 4–6 ft (1.3–1.8 m)
Food: They feed primarily on jellyfish.
Fact: Leatherback turtles lay their eggs on beaches.

A walrus

A leatherback turtle

FACT FILE

Weight: 1.3–2.2 tons
Length: 10–12 ft (3–3.6 m)
Food: It feeds mainly on worms, shellfish, sea-snails and shrimp.
Fact: The male walrus is twice the weight of the female.

A basking shark

FACT FILE

Weight: Up to 6 tons
Length: 33–49 ft (10–15 m)
Food: The basking shark uses a filter to consume as much plankton as it can.
Fact: It is the world's second largest fish.

What is the biggest sea animal

The huge blue whale is the largest animal on land or sea—ever. It weighs in at a massive 165 tons, has a heart the size of a small car and eats 6 tons of krill every day. The underwater song of the blue whale is louder than a jet plane!

Why do they migrate

Many species travel in search of food and breeding grounds. The great sea turtle swims thousands of kilometers to lay eggs on the same beach it was born on. Despite the weight of two skeletons (the shell counts as a second skeleton), the sea turtle is a great swimmer. The gray whale is thought to travel the greatest distance; its lifetime annual migration is up to 500,000 miles (800,000 km).

How do big animals feed

The bigger the animal, the more difficult it is for it to chase prey. Big animals tend to vacuum up plankton—and are called filter feeders—rather than attack fish. This makes feeding easier and gives them time to relax: the basking shark likes to "catch the rays" near the surface.

Which big animals are preyed on

Man is the only predator of most big sea creatures. One example is the sperm whale, which eats giant squid. The whale's stomach produces a sweet-smelling, precious substance called ambergris to counter the venom found in the squid's hard beak. Humans hunted the whale for centuries to collect this substance, and unfortunately, some species of large whales are listed as endangered.

How do they stay afloat

Most big sea animals have enormous oily organs that keep them afloat. Walruses—which are up to 12 ft (3.6 m) long and can weigh 1.3–2.2 tons—also have air bags in their throats. This helps them keep their heads above the water as they prowl the Arctic Ocean.

FACT FILE

A full-grown blue whale can gulp 50 tons of water in one go.

The giant squid has the largest eyes in the animal kingdom.

BRINGING UP BABY

Sea mammals are the only sea creatures that look after their young, but the rest have ingenious ways of protecting their eggs.

Why don't all sea creatures care for their young ❓

Most sea creatures produce thousands of eggs at a time—and fertilize them in the water, where ocean currents quickly whisk them away. This makes looking after eggs and the young impossible. Some animals do care for their eggs: the octopus stays with her eggs for two months until they hatch.

The female octopus stays with her eggs until they hatch

FACT FILE

Basking sharks are pregnant for 3.5 years and have the largest shark pups— 5.5 ft (1.6 m).

How do sea mammals rear their young

Sea mammals are pretty much like us humans: the females become pregnant and then give birth.
Whales and dolphins are pregnant for up to 18 months. Their "calves" can swim right after birth. The mothers care for their young for a year, feeding them milk and protecting them from predators.

A young dolphin will stay with its mother for a year

How do squid protect their eggs

Squid travel hundreds of miles to gather together in their hundreds of thousands to reproduce. The female releases millions of tiny eggs into the water. The eggs are then coated in a poisonous jelly. This protects them from the sharks, whales and dolphins that come to feast on the exhausted parents!

Squid migrating to reproduce

FACT FILE

The eggs of small sea creatures hatch as tiny larva and drift with the ocean currents. They are called plankton.

Whale and dolphin calves are a mottled color to camouflage them from predators.

The sea horse is the only animal in which the father "gets pregnant". The mother produces the eggs, but they are looked after in the father's body until they hatch. He carries them for about 50 days. The number of young released by the male sea horse ranges from 5 in some species to 1500 in others!

The whale shark has the largest egg in the world—it is 14 in. (36 cm) long. A shark egg is fertilized inside the womb but then hatches and grows there too. The shark "pup" survives by eating other eggs and pups. It swims away from the mother immediately after birth.

It is the male sea horse that becomes pregnant

HANDLE WITH CARE

Venom is the ultimate weapon in the war between predators and prey. These toxins are very powerful—as any unlucky swimmer who has come into contact with them may tell you!

Why are animals venomous

Venom is a great way for animals to protect themselves from predators—and a great way to attack prey too! The box jellyfish uses an incredibly powerful venom for both reasons. Its poison kills prey immediately. This stops the victim, caught up in the jellyfish's deadly, but delicate tentacles, from damaging them. Symptoms of a sting may include burning, swelling, breathing problems and sometimes even a heart attack.

A box jellyfish

How can you tell whether something is venomous

Unfortunately, life is tough when it comes to poison; you can't always tell whether the animal is venomous or not. The stonefish is well camouflaged and easy to step on—but it is also extremely deadly! Color is sometimes a warning: the small, blue-ringed octopus can bite through a wetsuit and kill in minutes.

FACT FILE

The colorful lionfish has stunning fins and spines. On the coral reef, however, it's the ultimate bully—pushing smaller fish into corners before stinging them to death.

Only the size of a golf ball, the blue-ringed octopus is lethal to humans

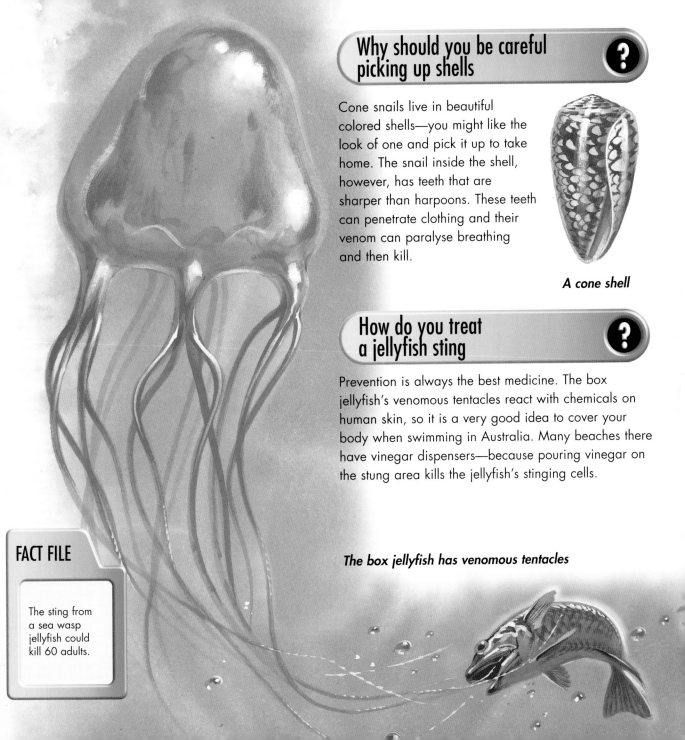

Why should you be careful picking up shells ❓

Cone snails live in beautiful colored shells—you might like the look of one and pick it up to take home. The snail inside the shell, however, has teeth that are sharper than harpoons. These teeth can penetrate clothing and their venom can paralyse breathing and then kill.

A cone shell

How do you treat a jellyfish sting ❓

Prevention is always the best medicine. The box jellyfish's venomous tentacles react with chemicals on human skin, so it is a very good idea to cover your body when swimming in Australia. Many beaches there have vinegar dispensers—because pouring vinegar on the stung area kills the jellyfish's stinging cells.

The box jellyfish has venomous tentacles

FACT FILE

The sting from a sea wasp jellyfish could kill 60 adults.

SCIENCE AND THE SEA

The story of Earth's past, present and future can be read in the oceans. Everything from the fate of dolphins to cures for disease may be hiding in the depths.

Why study sea creatures

Life evolved from the ocean, so to understand our past properly we need to look at ocean animals. Ocean life is more sensitive to change than life on land, so studying sea creatures allows us to see the changes caused by pollution—and stop them before they cause more harm.

How can they help improve human health

Scientists often call the ocean a "living laboratory" because sea animals can be studied quite easily. Sea animals are built more simply than land animals, so scientists can find out how living tissue works and why organs go wrong. Research on sharks has led to better blood pressure and heart drugs in humans.

How do scientists study sea creatures

Scientists trawl up marine animal specimens in trawler nets. They also use cameras on remote control vehicles to get pictures of deep-ocean creatures. Scientists can even go to the depths themselves in submarines called "submersibles". These machines have robotic arms and special equipment to bring live specimens to the surface.

FACT FILE

Ocean currents greatly affect Earth's climate.

Satellite images of the oceans tell us lots about changing weather patterns.

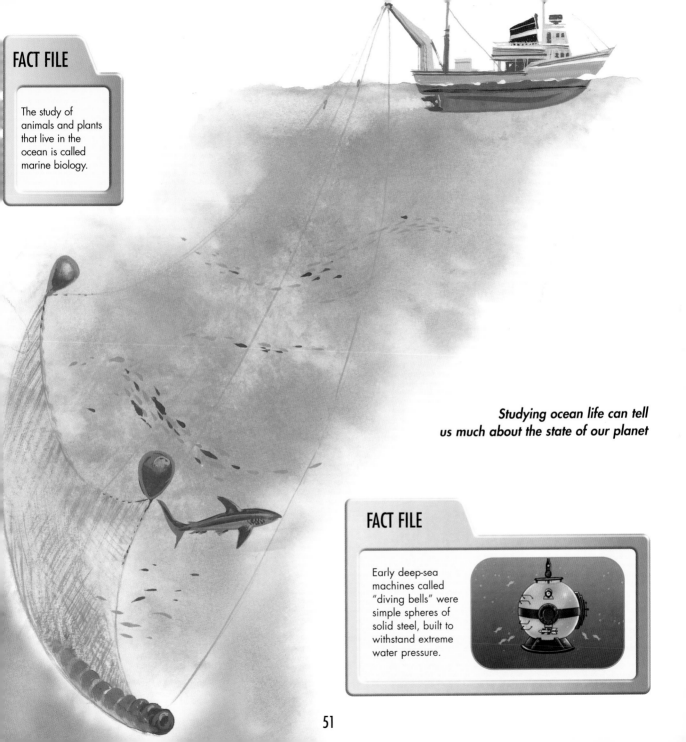

*Studying ocean life can tell
us much about the state of our planet*

51

What are the scientists working on now ?

Quite a lot is known about 50,000 marine species—but there may be another 1,500,000 to find out about! Small fish called minnows are helping develop drugs that can treat children with lead poisoning. Keeping an eye on the effects of environmental change on ocean creatures is very important too.

Marine biologists study ocean life

Remote control vehicles help us to explore the ocean

THE RESOURCEFUL OCEAN

Next time you eat fish sticks or use gas heating, remember that these good things come from the sea. The ocean is the world's greatest natural resource.

How much fish do we catch

Fish is highly nutritious and the major source of animal protein for humans. The fishing industry provides millions of jobs worldwide. Each year 70 to 75 million tons of fish are caught—that's the weight of 1,618 *Titanic* ships. It is important that fish populations are conserved by regulating overfishing and pollution.

An enormous amount of fish is caught each year

Where are fish caught

Most fish are caught in parts of the ocean called "upwellings". In an upwelling, deep-ocean water meets a "coastal shelf" (the part of a landmass that is underwater). This sends plankton-rich water to the surface. The Peruvian upwelling is the richest—it contains 66,000 times more fish than the open ocean.

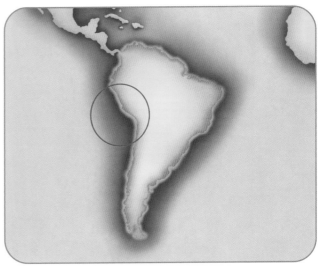

The ocean around Peru contains many fish

How long will fish last

We are catching so many fish every year that we could easily drain the oceans of fish within 20 years. This is partly because of the "drift nets" used by huge fishing trawlers. These nets trap everything that's in the water—all the way from the surface to the sea floor.

What is modern fishing like

For centuries, little fishing boats would set out from coastal villages every night. They would catch small loads close to shore. Nowadays, enormous, mechanized ships called trawlers fish the ocean far from shore. They use fish-seeking radar to catch 350 tons of fish in one go.

What other ocean resources are there

Fish aren't the only resource in the ocean. There are oil, gas and mineral deposits hidden under the sea floor. The ocean is also a great resource for all sorts of tourism, from beach vacations to leisure boats. Using these resources inevitably means harming or destroying the places where sea animals live.

FACT FILE

The first marine parks are now open. These protect specific ocean environments from fishing and other industries.

A trawler is used to catch several tons of fish

The ocean is a wonderful resource, but humans must take greater care of it. Man-made pollution could lead to the death of many of the ocean's creatures

ENDANGERED SPECIES

When the members of an animal species die faster than they reproduce, the species can become extinct. Humans are making this happen all the time—how can we stop this from happening?

What sea animals are endangered species

Unfortunately, there are hundreds of marine animals on the endangered species list, including six types of whale and three types of shark. Amongst other species, you will find the spotted dolphin, the manatee, the dugong, all eight types of sea turtle, the sea otter and the queen conch.

What can we do to save animals

Some endangered species recover their numbers, whilst others disappear forever. There is little we can do once numbers fall beyond a certain point. However, we can help by making it illegal to kill endangered creatures and by breeding them in captivity. Fishermen can use special nets that allow them to escape.

FACT FILE

All species of sea turtles are listed as threatened or endangered. This is partly due to accidental fishing and a demand for tortoiseshell.

Why are species endangered

Throughout time, species have become extinct, which means "died out". Scientists estimate that over 90% of the species that ever existed have become extinct. Recently, however, it has been humans that have been causing many of these extinctions. This is because we have been over-hunting or over-fishing, destroying natural habitats and polluting the environment.

A trapped dolphin

All of these animals are currently listed as endangered

A sea otter

A spotted dolphin

A gray whale

A sea turtle

A manatee

A dugong

A queen conch

A bowhead whale

Which is the cutest endangered sea animal

Sea otters are sleek and furry and 4 ft (1.3 m) long. They spend most of their time in Pacific Ocean bays cracking open clams on rocks. They are fast and graceful swimmers. Numbers of sea otters were originally estimated at 150,000–300,000. However, they were hunted for their fur between 1741 and 1911 and oil spills also caused their fur to lose its waterproof quality, which means that the otter then dies of the cold. The population consequently fell to 1,000–2,000. A ban on hunting and conservation efforts were introduced, which helped to boost the population, but the sea otter is still classified as an endangered species.

How many whales are left

Even though most whale hunting has now stopped, some species will never recover. There are less than 4,000 right whales left—they were heavily hunted because they were easy to catch and they floated after being killed. There are about 10,000 bowheads, 12,000 blues, 13,000 humpbacks and 18,000 gray whales.

FACT FILE

Gray whales were called "devilfish" by whalers because they fought so ferociously for their lives. They have a layer of blubber up to 10 in. (25 cm) thick.

What is a coelacanth

The coelacanth (below) is a 380-million year old fish, and was thought to have become extinct with the dinosaurs—but then turned up in the Indian Ocean!

The coelacanth turned up in the Indian Ocean, after it was believed to be extinct

FISHY FACTS

You might find some of these fantastic fishy facts hard to believe—but they are all absolutely true!

Which are the fastest fish ?

The swordfish and marlin reach speeds of 75 mph (120 km/h), leaving the sailfish trailing behind. It reaches a top speed of 68 mph (110 km/h), folding its fins—even the biggest—into its body to move quicker. The third fastest fish is the 55 mph (88-km/h) bluefin tuna.

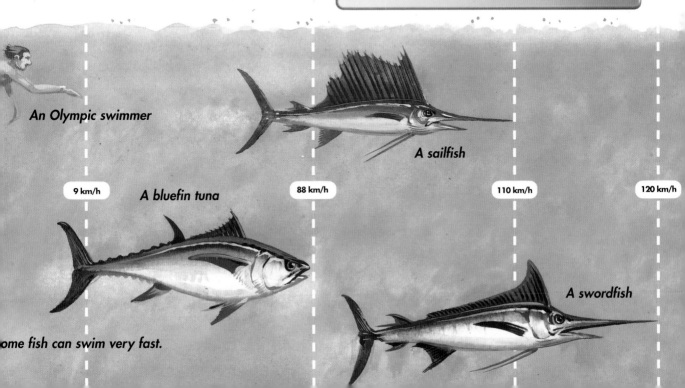

An Olympic swimmer

A sailfish

9 km/h

A bluefin tuna

88 km/h

110 km/h

120 km/h

A swordfish

Some fish can swim very fast.

How small can sea creatures be

Plankton and sea bacteria are the smallest sea creatures of all—and they are microscopic. Just one mouthful of seawater contains millions of bacteria and hundreds of thousands of plankton. The famous White Cliffs of Dover in the UK are made from billions of fossilized plankton. The word "plankton" comes from a Greek word meaning "drifting".

How bizarre does fish behavior get

The four-winged flying fish flies over the waves for 3,280 ft (1,000 m). Starfish eat by sliding their stomachs into their prey. The porcupine fish turns into a prickly balloon when it is attacked; dead sharks have been found with puffed-up porcupine fish still stuck in their throats.

A porcupine fish

Some sea creatures are microscopic

A four-winged flying fish

What are some amazing ocean facts ?

The ocean is an amazing place with some incredible statistics. The world's oceans produce just over 70% of Earth's oxygen. The ocean deep goes 6.86 miles (11 km) down, while the top of Mount Everest is only 5.49 miles (8.8 km) high. The longest mountain range in the known universe lies deep in the ocean. It is 40,000 miles (64,372 km) long.

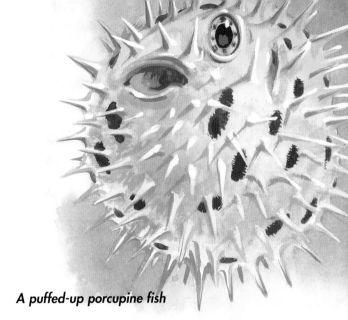

A puffed-up porcupine fish

Who finds the strangest uses for fish ?

The ancient Greeks applied electric rays to their bodies to numb the pain of childbirth. Shark eyes are used in human eye transplants.
The pufferfish is extremely poisonous—the liver is 1,000 times deadlier than cyanide—but considered a delicacy in Japan.

A sting ray tail used on a spear

The ocean is deeper, in places, than the height of Mount Everest

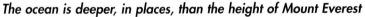

GLOSSARY

Abyssopelagic

The 13,000 to 19,680 ft depth zone of the ocean.

Ambergris

A pale gray, waxy substance with a strong smell produced in the intestines of sperm whales, found in lumps floating on the water or washed ashore.

Ampullae

The ampullae of Lorenzini are electroreceptive organs positioned in the head of a shark. These electrical field sensing devices are jelly-filled pores which enable a shark to detect the presence of another living creature even if all its other senses are deactivated.

Atoll

A ring-shaped coral reef surrounding a lagoon.

Coastal shelf

The part of a landmass that is under the water.

Coelacanth

The 400 million-year-old fossil fish which predates the dinosaurs; and is the closest link between fish and the first amphibian creatures which made the transition from sea to land in the Devonian period. It was first discovered in 1938.

Diving bell

A large, hollow, bottomless, underwater container pumped full of air, to which an unequipped diver returns to take in oxygen.

Dugong

A gray-brown, whale-like, plant-eating tropical sea mammal that lives for up to 50 years and grows up to 10 ft in length.

Epipelagic zone

The 0 to 656 ft depth zone of the ocean.

Food chain

A sequence of organisms arranged in such a way that each feeds on the organism below it in the chain, and serves as a source of food for the organism above it.

Gravitational pull

This is what causes waves and tides, because as the Moon moves around Earth it pulls water upwards on the near side of Earth and downwards on the far side; but the downforce is weaker.

Hadalpelagic zone

The 19,680 ft plus depth zone of the ocean.

Invertebrates

Any animal lacking a backbone.

Krill

A tiny, shrimp-like shellfish or crustacean, around 0.6 to 1.2 in. long, that is eaten by whales. Krill is a Norwegian word, meaning whale food.

Logarithmic spiral

As in the nautilus snail where each new chamber of its shell is a fixed percentage larger than the previous one.

GLOSSARY

Mariana Trench

This is located in the Pacific Ocean not far from Japan. It is the deepest part of Earth's oceans and the deepest location of Earth itself. Its deepest point is called the Challenger Deep.

Mesopalagic zone

The 656 to 3,300 ft depth zone of the ocean.

Narwhal

An Arctic whale; the male has a long, spiral tusk.

Nudibranch

Also known as sea slugs because they are like snails without shells. Many are brightly colored, others are more subtly colored and therefore easily camouflaged. They are some of the most beautiful creatures in the ocean and there are some 3,000 different species.

Pangaea

The name given to the hypothetical "supercontinent" that is thought to have represented the entire landmass of Earth about 200 to 250 million years ago; before it split into separate continents.

Panthalassa

The ocean that surrounded the surface of Earth hundreds of millions of years ago before it divided into five oceans.

Photosynthesis

A process whereby green plants manufacture carbohydrates from carbon dioxide and water using the light energy from sunlight trapped by the pigment chlorophyll.

Plankton

Microscopic animals and plants that float or drift with the current in the surface waters of seas and lakes. Plankton are an important food source for invertebrates, fish and whales and form the basis of all marine food chains.

Pod

This is the name given to the closely-knit family groups of killer (orca) whales which consist of up to 30 members. They swim together, usually no more than 0.6 miles apart.

Primeval

Something that belongs to Earth's beginnings; in other words, from the earliest age or ages.

ROVs

Remotely operated vehicles.

Submersible

A vessel that is able to operate successfully under water.

Symbiosis

The close association between two organisms of different species, usually to the benefit of both partners. Mostly this relationship is essential for their mutual survival.

Trilobite

An extinct marine arthropod having a flat, oval body divided lengthwise into three sections. Also, the fossilized remains of this animal.

Upwellings

Caused by a process in which cold, often nutrient-rich water from the ocean depths rises to the surface.

INDEX